DIPLOMATIC LIFE

DIPLOMATIC LIFE

A Rose with Thorns

VERA TANGER, WITH SANDRA AMARO

iUniverse, Inc.
Bloomington

Diplomatic Life
A Rose with Thorns

iUniverse books may be ordered through booksellers or by contacting:

iUniverse
1663 Liberty Drive
Bloomington, IN 47403
www.iuniverse.com
1-800-Authors (1-800-288-4677)

ISBN: 978-1-4759-7864-3 (sc)
ISBN: 978-1-4759-7866-7 (hc)
ISBN: 978-1-4759-7865-0 (ebk)

Printed in the United States of America

iUniverse rev. date: 04/11/2013

Contents

Preface

Do you often find yourself in formal situations with little idea of what is acceptable to do or say? Do you often find yourself struggling to know what is appropriate to wear? Do you need to know how to set a formal table?

If you can identify with these or similar questions about etiquette, then this book was written for people like you who feel inadequate and need guidance and clarification on this highly specialized subject.

Although more common in the world of diplomats, these issues are not exclusive and are often relevant in the business world too. Despite interpersonal communication being more casual nowadays, formal etiquette can always come in handy. You may have to host a large gathering or business function, or find yourself in the company of guests or clients from a different culture. You will find that having a few tips on how to make formal introductions or how to organize seating will make these tasks less daunting.

You will learn the answers to these and many more related questions you may have about appropriate formal behavior. This book will help you to discover ways to overcome most, if not all, of your etiquette dilemmas and will become your concise, easy-to-use, go-to bible on matters of diplomacy. Knowing the rules of etiquette and protocol will provide you with enough knowledge to act and react appropriately in any situation.

Introduction

> Etiquette is the science of living. It embraces everything. It is ethics. It is honor.
>
> —Emily Post

> Good manners are just a way of showing people that we have respect for them.
>
> —Bill Kelly

Protocol is a set of rules that defines hierarchy, establishes orders of precedence at social and political functions in accordance with professional rank, and determines forms of address as well as certain regulations for official functions.

Etiquette is comprised of concepts of ethics, costumes, traditions, and good manners. Together, protocol and etiquette provide a universal language for accepted practices in most situations, although a good dose of common sense is often also required.

Nobody is born knowing how to behave. I was lucky enough to have been born into a family where some of these practices were common to our everyday existence. In 1981, after arriving in China for my first posting abroad, I quickly understood that living in the diplomatic world involves procedures beyond the ones I learned growing up. Asking around was not enough to learn what to do and how to do it. I started reading books and manuals to broaden my knowledge, which I could then apply to my new life. But the few existing texts were either out of print, anecdotal life experiences, or dealt exclusively with state protocol. The nitty-gritty and practical aspects of everyday diplomatic life were never mentioned.

I decided to write a manual to pass on my life experiences and the knowledge that I had gathered in a down-to-earth, hands-on way.

I asked Sandra Amaro, also a diplomat's wife, to join me on this project and she added suggestions that enriched the discussion. I would also like to include a very special thank you to my husband, who, besides being a great supporter and mentor, gave me this opportunity in life due to his profession.

This book endeavors to explain and clarify in everyday language the most important details for the most common situations. To further clarify concepts and situations and to simplify reading, I have incorporated illustrations and images.

Diplomatic Life: A Rose with Thorns

There is more to diplomatic life than meets the eye. Living in different countries is the most visible and the most interesting side of it. The glamour of bygone days is no longer there, but this life allows you to meet top-level people like scientists, artists, politicians and free thinkers, to name a few and enjoy social prerogatives one would not otherwise enjoy. Presently, security is a real issue in many countries of the world and, for those traveling with the family this has become a serious concern.

Living abroad as a diplomat's spouse/partner

It is not so easy to work abroad, and in most cases requires some preexisting bilateral agreements as well as speaking the local language. Spouses with a professional career of their own in their home country often think twice before accompanying the officer abroad. Becoming known only as the "wife/husband/ partner of . . ." or the "mother/father of . . ." is sometimes hard to accept. Some even feel a loss of identity. On top of this, their financial independence is gone. Having to ask for money to pay for a simple cup of coffee can become an issue with serious consequences. The spouse's decision to stay in the home country or accompany the diplomat abroad is the moment of truth for many couples, and unfortunately there is no middle ground. Either they grow together and endure the tensions, or they split and end up in divorce. This has changed the diplomatic family, and more and more, the diplomat travels alone.

For those who decide to accompany the diplomatic officer, it might be interesting to use this period of time to think about what makes you happy and what you would really like to do. Be flexible and keep an open mind. Enjoy the traveling and learn about new cultures and peoples. Fantastic novel writers and creative artists as well as experienced event organizers have emerged during such periods. Seeing the good side of every situation with a positive attitude will help you to overcome obstacles.

The "global nomads"

Due to the requirements of diplomatic life, the diplomat's children live abroad, often attending a foreign language school and having to change schools often. They become children of the world and, as Robin Pascoe calls them, "global nomads." Their parents are the only family they know and the only permanent pillars in their lives. Even in an age of Skype or Google, leaving friends behind can be very distressing for a teen.

 The way a child's parents react to the news of a new posting will affect the child's reaction too. To help overcome the difficulties you may encounter, interact with the child/children as much as possible, do activities together, and create a strong bond while getting to know the country you are in.

Coming back home

As strange as it may sound, coming back home can be more stressful than any posting abroad. Things have changed at home, and you have changed! Your friends will seem different to you, mostly because you have gained a worldly outlook and they have not. Unfortunately, this is reality.

In addition to the domestic culture shock, for most diplomats there is a substantial reduction in salary, and making ends meet becomes an issue. On the other hand, the diplomat's spouse may rejoin the workforce and become a paid professional once again.

Personal and Professional Image

Fifteen seconds

It only takes fifteen seconds to make an impression, which is the perception others have of us, not the idea we have of ourselves. There really is no second chance for a first impression. According to a study by Albert Mehrabian, well known for his publications on the importance of verbal and nonverbal messages, when people make an assessment of us, 55 percent of their impression comes from our visual appearance, 38 percent from our voice, and only 7 percent comes from what we say. It doesn't sound fair and many times does not even correspond to reality, but this is human nature, and diplomats are humans too. Bear in mind that diplomats and their families represent a country, and their image will reflect on that country. Be conscious of your behavior at all times, particularly in smaller communities where one is easily spotted.

One's personal and professional image is based on clothing, body language and facial expression, posture, and gestures. Dress conservatively and appropriately for the occasion. Choose clothes that best fit your body shape and age group and respect local customs. Wearing a miniskirt in a Muslim country or shorts for a reception is inappropriate and does not look right. Wearing makeup and jewelry is nice and after a certain age is almost mandatory, but use it in moderation. Simplicity is beautiful.

Personal hygiene is important. Be wary of body odors, especially bad breath. Keep your hair clean, with no visible roots if you color it. Your hands should be clean and dry and always ready for a handshake. Men should shave every day or keep a well-groomed beard.

Enter a room with confidence, walking tall with your arms hanging alongside your body. While talking to others, making introductions, or giving speeches or presentations, remove your hands from your pockets. Use your arms and hands wisely, and don't raise them above your head or make exaggerated movements. Sit up straight and only cross your legs at informal gatherings. Stand up when greeting others, and make eye contact and smile when shaking hands or greeting in any other way. It is better to avoid any hand gestures, as they differ greatly from culture to culture. What may seem innocent in one country can be offensive in another.

Speak slowly using a normal tone of voice, and pronounce words carefully. Others may not speak a foreign language well, and it is impolite to exclude them from the conversation. Don't speak with food in your mouth, and never chew gum in public.

Answer the phone politely and with a smile. If you don't speak the local language, excuse yourself in English, as some words will always be understood on the other side.

Who goes ahead?

In some countries women follow men, while in others men will give passage to women in doorways or when entering an elevator. On the other hand, in order to help women in case they fall, men should go first when going down the stairs and after when going up. No matter your gender, always hold the door open until you have passed through, allowing the person coming behind you to grab it from you, and always help handicapped people or anyone with difficulty. Being polite is still free and appreciated anywhere in the world.

The Appropriate Attire

Got an invitation and don't know what to wear?

Dressing appropriately for an occasion is important. Standing out in a crowd because you have on the wrong outfit is embarrassing. You want to blend in with the crowd.

Times have changed, and the level of formality is not as strict as it used to be; however, some rules still apply. Acknowledge and take into consideration the ways of the country in which you are living. For example, Paris is more formal than Vilnius, and in hot countries or seasons, rules tend to be more relaxed too. Generally speaking, one dresses light in the morning; as the day progresses, the attire becomes more sophisticated and formal, peaking at dinners and evening parties.

On the other hand, the hostess should never be overdressed, as her guests will either think they didn't read the invitation correctly or don't know how to dress properly.

There are three main designations: **Casual, Informal** and **Formal,** but for less formal occasions, **Smart Casual** (no tie for men) is being introduced.

Casual, Business Casual (UK/USA)
Tenue informelle (FR)
Traje de Passeio, Blazer, Business Casual (PT)
Informal (SP)

Among the diplomatic community, or unless otherwise stated on the invitation card, casual wear applies to working breakfasts, social coffee mornings, lunches and afternoon teas, daytime meetings, and some receptions. Attending modern music concerts or any other form of artistic life and sometimes dinners during the summer implies dressing with no tie for men.

Male
Sports jacket/blazer and pants
Tie or bow tie (exceptions made for an open-collar shirt)
Dress shoes or loafers

Female
Skirt/pants with blouse or sporty jacket
Pumps or flats
Medium handbag
Some jewelry and light makeup

Informal, Dark suit, Business suit (UK/USA)
Tenue de Ville (FR)
Fato Escuro (PT)
Traje oscuro (SP)

Informal or sometimes semiformal wear may be worn for cocktail parties, official lunches and dinners, classical music events, openings and evening receptions, and mainly National Day celebrations.

Male
Solid navy or charcoal business suit
Tie or bow tie
White shirt for official evening occasions
Dress dark shoes and socks

Female
Jacket with pants/skirt or short cocktail dress
Medium-heeled shoes or dressy flats
Medium handbag
Some jewelry and light makeup

If the usage of hat/fascinator is required, it should be mentioned on the invitation.

Formal, Tuxedo (USA)
Black Tie/Dinner Jacket/Formal (UK)
Smoking/Cravate Noire (FR)
Smoking (PT)
Esmoquin (SP)

Formal wear is worn at very formal dinners (state visits) and evening affairs such as the opera or balls. This information should be stated on the invitation, but when in doubt, it is safer to ask the organizing party.

Male
Black tuxedo with wing collar, white shirt with cuff links
Bow tie and matching cummerbund or vest/waistcoat
Black oxford shoes
Black socks, preferably knee high
White scarf (optional)

Note: For a two- to four-button jacket, leave the last button undone

Female
Long ball gown or long skirt and top
High-heeled shoes
Pochette or clutch
Makeup and jewelry
Stylish hair

White-tie, Tailcoat (UK/USA)
Habit Noir/Cravate Blanche/Tenue de Gala (FR)
Casaca (PT)
Frac (SP)

This designation is only used at very particular events, and it should always be mentioned on the invitation. The vest is black for daytime events such as the ceremony for the presentation of credential letters and white for evening events, except for religious ceremonies at the Vatican (Holy See) where only black is worn. Since this is not commonly used anymore, it is customary to rent this outfit from a good-quality store.

Male
Black tailcoat and matching trousers
White piqué vest
White piqué bow tie
Wing collar white shirt
Black patent leather court shoes
Black socks, preferably knee high

Female
Long ball gown or long skirt and top
High heel shoes
Pochette or clutch
Makeup and jewelry
Stylish hair

Uniform (USA/UK)
Uniforme (FR/PT/SP)

The gala uniform is mostly used by the armed forces personnel at National Day celebrations. The diplomatic uniform may be used at the presentation ceremony of credential letters and in accordance with the local protocol department.

Cutaway (USA)
Morning Coat (UK)
Jacquette/Tenue de Cerimonie du Matin (FR)
Fraque (PT)
Chaqué (ESP)

A cutaway or morning coat is only used at formal weddings celebrated at lunchtime, when groom also wears it. Since it is not a commonly used outfit, it is customary to rent from a good-quality store.

<u>Male</u>
Morning coat complete suit*
White shirt with cuff links
Tie and matching vest (light silver grey is classic)
Black oxford shoes and socks
* Coat is used unbuttoned

<u>Female</u>
Short colorful dress with jacket or shawl
High-heeled shoes
Pochette or clutch
Makeup and jewelry
Stylish hair

If mentioned on the invitation card, ladies may wear a hat or fascinator.

Decorations are worn on the left lapel or the top left side of the dress or uniform and the band is put on the right shoulder and across the chest.

Introductions and Addressing Others

Who is introduced to whom?

This is a common question with an easy answer: the person of lower professional rank is introduced to the higher-ranked person. If you are doing the introduction, face the highest-ranking person and pronounce the other party's name in a way that may easily be understood by the other, slowly and clearly, followed by a few words about the person.

For example: "Ambassador Simpson, may I introduce you to Mr. Peter Crawford, first secretary of the XXX Embassy; Mrs. Anne Bloomberg (CEO), I would like to introduce you to Mr. John Clark, the General Manager of ABC Hardware Company and the guest speaker on our next conference".

Both smile, shake hands or greet each other in the polite way, and say "How do you do?" or "Hello Mr. Crawford." It is now up to the highest-ranking person to start a conversation.

Meeting different people is an everyday affair, especially when you are a newcomer, and putting faces to names is a difficult task. Use every opportunity to repeat the newly introduced person's name throughout the conversation—"Yes, Mr. Crawford," or "I don't know, Peter"—and say it three times mentally. This is a good memory technique. Also, whenever you mention that person to anyone else, always mention their name and surname too.

If you see the person you're speaking with, struggling to remember your name, help them a little by saying something like, "I'm Theresa Jones. We met at the Venezuelan National Day reception." It is a nice icebreaker and certainly helps.

Social introductions use gender (ladies first), age, professional rank and title as a rule.

Always stand for introductions and greetings. Remove your hands from pockets, show respect for others and smile.

When a lady enters a room, every man should stand up, but ladies, particularly older ones, don't have to stand for men unless the men are higher in rank or are religious officials. This may be common knowledge but always remember to follow local traditions, as failure to do so may be seen as rudeness and lack of respect.

What do I call someone?

Addressing others is an important aspect and varies greatly depending on job, gender, age, position, from country to country as well as between cultures. "What shall I call so-and-so?" is a question that is asked many times. If one does not know exactly what is appropriate, it is always better to be more formal than less. Start by using a more formal approach and only change it if and when told otherwise.

Among same-rank diplomats nowadays, it is widely accepted and very common to be on a first-name basis. The tendency is to forget which exact person one is talking about so, mentally repeating their full name a few times may be a useful memory tool.

When meeting an ambassador, particularly if you happen to be lower in rank, use the form "Mr. or Madam Ambassador" or "Ambassador Andersen." Only use his or her first name after being told that it is okay to do so. Among ambassadors, this may also apply due to age difference or another particular deference.

For an ambassador's wife, always start formally. Use Mrs. and the surname or, if posted in an informal country, use her first name, but respectfully. Only use her first name if you are among equals. Again, remember the surname!

Nowadays, ambassador's wives carry personal cards with their name, phone, mobile number, and e-mail address. The majority use their country's coat of arms too (if allowed by their own country's protocol procedures), making it easier to identify which country they are representing.

The term "Excellency," when referring to ambassadors is rarely used nowadays in the spoken language but more so in writing.

When using the English language, addressing everybody as *you* is easy, but it's not so in other languages like German or French, for example. *Herr/Monsieur* or *Frau/Madame* followed by the surname and the third person form *Sie/vous* is considered the proper way of addressing others, no matter their rank. The second person form *Du/tu* is the familiar and less formal way, and is only used after being told to do so or among same-rank colleagues.

In some places, like Portuguese speaking countries or India, the use of one's academic title before the surname is also important and is something people can be sensitive about. Ask around to see what is the norm, and respect the host country's ways.

Address household employees according to local rules and do not become too familiar and intimate with them. Always show them respect. While speaking to them with reference to your spouse, use "Mr. or Mrs. Smith" rather than John or Mary.

What follow are the most common forms of address, which may vary from country to country and according to local tradition. When addressing anyone formally, use the direct form when speaking to them directly e.g. Your Highness. Use the indirect form when speaking about them in the third person, e.g. His or Her Highness.

	Direct form	Indirect form
President	Your Excellency	His/Her Excellency
Emperor, King, Queen	Your Majesty	His/Her Majesty
Prince, Princess	Your Royal Highness	His/Her Royal Highness
Cabinet Ministers (in some English-speaking countries)	The Honorable Minister for . . .	
Mayor (in some English-speaking countries)	Your Worship	His/Her Worship
Pope	Your Holiness	His Holiness
Cardinal	Your Eminence	His Eminence
Archbishop	Your Grace	His Grace
Bishop	Your Excellency	His Excellency
Priest	Father/ the Reverend	Father
Ambassador	Mr. Ambassador or Ambassador + surname	His Excellency
Lady ambassador	Madame Ambassador or Ambassador + surname	Her Excellency
Wife/husband of an ambassador	Mr./Mrs. + surname, unless they have an academic title of their own	

Forms of Greeting

Greetings acknowledge another person's presence and are internationally accepted as a golden rule of politeness. Smile and say "Hello, Mr. Jones," or introduce yourself if needed. This first contact is very important and needs to create a good first impression.

In the Western world, men shake hands with other men and women and among themselves also use the handshake, particularly for first-time and for formal introductions. As they become more familiar and depending on the country and local culture, women tend to give social kisses. These vary in quantity—one kiss (Argentina), two kisses (most countries), and three kisses (Balkans, Belgium)—as well as which side to start on—right (most countries), left (Italy). In Arab countries, men tend to hold hands upon the handshake and keep talking for a while; in Russia, men kiss each other. Before going abroad, learn the customs of the country and use the local greeting form with host country nationals as soon as possible.

The handshake has gone global and is widely used with foreigners in countries where the local greeting differs, such as in Japan or India.

In any circumstance, if a woman accepts the social kiss as a greeting, it is up to her to initiate the procedure. Otherwise she should extend her hand, clearly stating her preference for the handshake, or just nod.

Circumstances may not allow for a verbal greeting, such as during religious services, conferences, concerts, etc. Remember to wave or nod gently and smile in these situations to show some sort of recognition and, if possible, greet people properly and talk for a while later.

The distance between people while socializing, as well as the need for eye contact, may vary significantly by culture. In the West, eye contact is a must, whereas it is not so in the East. Ask, read about and show interest in different cultures. People love to inform and be helpful.

Rules for a handshake

For a proper handshake, use the right hand and hold it firmly, communicating positive energy and showing the right attitude.

Strength—The handshake has to be firm and decisive, neither too soft nor too hard, neither slippery nor a bone crusher. Remember to use less pressure when greeting somebody standing in a greeting line. Your handshake will be one of many.

Parallel hands—Make sure your hand is flat with the thumb up and parallel to the other person's hand. This shows equality. The palm facing down represents authority and dominance; facing up means subservience.

Standing—Always stand up for a handshake, no matter the gender. In the past and on social occasions, women did not rise for a greeting, but nowadays, only older ladies are excused.

Dry and clean—Cover a cough or sneeze with your left hand, keeping your right hand always clean and ready for a handshake as well as for holding food and drink at receptions and cocktails.

Duration—Hold a handshake for two to three seconds and "pump" it two or three times. Smile and remember what is locally perceived as acceptable.

Eye contact—A must in the West, eye contact is to be avoided between men and women in Arab countries and kept short in Eastern cultures.

Smile—Always! But respect the local etiquette, customs and traditions.

Hands loose—Keep your arms alongside your body and your hands out of your pockets when greeting somebody, talking to another person, making a speech, or speaking in front of an audience. In body language terms, it simply shows that you have nothing to hide and feel self-confident.

Hand-kissing—A kiss on the hand is a beautiful compliment and sign of respect for married or older ladies but has lately fallen into disuse. A woman extends her hand to the man, who will slightly lower his head while holding her hand and make the gesture of kissing it.

In Catholic countries, it is customary for men to bow or women to do a small curtsy while kissing the ecclesiastical ring when greeting high members of the church such as bishops, cardinals, and the Pope.

Royals

Monarchies have very specific rules that vary from country to country, although they are catching up with modern times. More and more, the handshake, along with a ceremonial neck bow (from the head) for men and a small curtsy for women, is becoming acceptable.

In Malaysia, for example, you would put your hands together and raise them to the monarch's forehead. In Saudi Arabia, both men and women shake hands, and then only when the monarch extends his hand first.

Handling Business Cards

Meeting people and exchanging business cards is a very common practice among professionals and diplomats are no exception.

Understanding different cultures means understanding etiquette and the exchanging of business cards varies culturally. In some countries, such as India, titles are given great importance, or in China the use of golden characters is seen as auspicious. Pay attention to these details and follow the local rule.

Professional business cards should have:

- Coat of arms of owner's country
- Name by which the person is known
- Rank or position at the embassy or international company
- Forms of contact: professional address, phone number, cell phone (if applicable)
- e-mail (if applicable)

For security reasons, don't print your home address or private number on the card, but you can handwrite it on the card if appropriate. In countries with different alphabets, it is customary to translate and print double-faced cards for easier understanding.

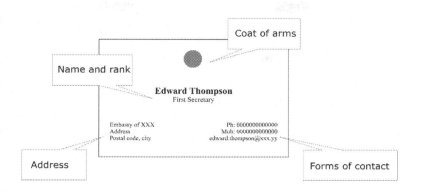

Business cards reflect the owner's attitude and self-image; therefore, keep yours clean and in a cardholder within easy reach. Searching through pockets and handbags for your card gives a sloppy impression.

With your right hand (or in Asia, with both hands) present the card with the print facing the recipient. Always receive a card in the way you were given it. For example, if someone offers the card with both hands, accept it with both hands and give your card the same way. Allow for the highest-ranking person to initiate the exchange; however, with people of equal rank, you may offer a card first, keeping in mind that giving a business card is an invitation for the other person to contact you. Choose carefully.

After receiving the card, take a moment to glance at it, showing some respect and interest and never write any comments on it in front of the donor. Carefully place it in your wallet, briefcase, or handbag, or on top of your desk, but never in your back pocket. Once in private, you may write some notes on it, such as the person's physical characteristics or the topic spoken about, as a personal reminder.

Due to frequent changes in a diplomat's life, avoid printing too many cards for yourself at one time so as to keep all information up to date.

When sending flowers, a book, a bottle of wine, or any other gift, include your professional card, and to be courteous, handwrite the name of your spouse or partner and cross out your professional title and surname, as shown on the example. Some words may be added, but never sign your own card. Use blue or black ink only, as other colors may be offensive or may have a different purpose, like red for corrections.

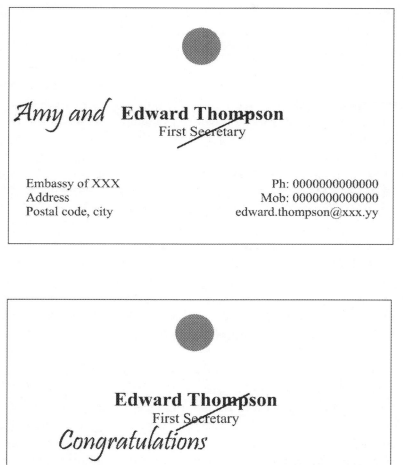

Protocol for Seating in Cars

Creating a good impression when traveling by car means knowing where to sit, how and when to enter the vehicle and how and when to exit.

Seats in cars driven by professional drivers are occupied according to rank and hierarchy. The prime seat is in the rear, on the opposite side from the driver (1), meaning on the right-hand side in countries where traffic drives on the right like the United States, Canada, European countries, and China, and on the left where traffic drives on the left like the United Kingdom, Malaysia, Japan, and Mozambique. Seat number two is on the left behind the driver's seat (2), and the third seat is next to the driver (3).

The doors of the vehicle should be held open by the driver, mainly for the highest-ranking person. He or she will enter the car through the right-hand door (in countries where traffic drives on the right-hand side). The official's aid/spouse/partner or accompanying person should enter the car first through the left-rear door and leave the car before the highest-ranking person.

In accordance with the host country's rules, the ambassador or his or her representative may have to be driven in the official car, using his or her country's flag. However, as soon as he or she leaves the car, the flag should be removed. If a long journey has to be made, in order not to damage the flag, it should only be placed on the car shortly before reaching the final destination. This is not so when taking part in official convoys.

As a host, remember to use the correct seat according to precedence. For example, the ambassador will occupy seat number two, leaving seat number one for the Minister, Secretary of State or important invited guest and the embassy's first secretary will take the front seat.

Seating according to rank:

Car with driver
1—The seat in the rear opposite to driver
2—The seat in the rear behind driver
3—The seat next to driver

Car with driver and personal security
1—The seat in the back opposite to driver
2—The seat in the back behind driver
(S)—Security—The seat next to driver

For security reasons, allow the bodyguard to open and close the car doors at any time.

Limousine
1—The seat in the back opposite to driver
2—The seat in the back behind the driver
3—The seat facing the highest-ranking person
4—The seat facing the second-highest-ranking person

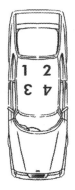

In the case where there are only three passengers, the lowest-ranking person should use seat number four, providing more legroom for the highest-ranking person.

Self-driven car
This is a topic about which opinions may differ. The best rule to go by is good common sense. Above all, do not offend the host country's traditions by trying to impose your cultural ways.

In the case where the car is driven by the owner, the order of seating should be:

1—The seat in front next to car owner
2—The seat in the back opposed to car owner
3—The seat in the back behind the car owner

If the driver happens to be a woman and there are other women in the group, allow the highest-ranking lady to take the front seat, while men will use the rear seats according to rank.

Invitation Cards

In the past, invitation cards were used as the invitation *per se*, but today they are more often used as a reminder—*pour mémoire* (p.m.). The procedure starts with a phone call. This is direct if no particular formalities are involved or you know the other person well, or via the secretary or personal assistant when there is a difference in rank or protocol. This procedure takes precedence. In the end, a phone call makes life easier, as the answer is given straight away.

The invitation should be printed on ecru or white cards, using black or dark blue elegant fonts such as Palace Script, Kunstler Script, or Lucida Calligraphy.

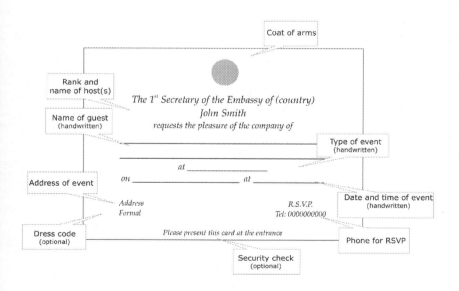

The necessary elements on the card are:

Country's coat of arms
Rank and title of host
Name and surname of host
Name and surname of host's spouse or partner, when applicable
Rank, name, and surname of guest
Event description*: lunch, dinner, reception, cocktail, etc.
Date and time of the event
Address where event will take place
Dress code (optional)
Phone number for RSVP
Security check (optional)

* For events with a long guest list, such as a National Day celebration, a farewell reception, or a cultural event of any kind, it is customary to print a special invitation card with a description of the event printed. For security reasons and in order to avoid uninvited guests trying to gain access (believe it or not, it happens often), presenting this invitation card at the entrance may be required. If so, include this detail on the invitation so that guests know to bring the card for verification by the welcoming party.

A separate page with location map may be added when needed.

The layout

This is the layout traditionally used for an invitation card.

(Coat of arms)

On the occasion of the National Day
the Ambassador of (country)
Mr. Peter Brown
requests the pleasure of the company of

(rank and name of guest) _____

_____

at a Reception
on Monday, October 2nd, from 7.30 pm to 10.00 pm

Address of event location   Regrets only
City   (Phone number for reply)

Italic—handwritten

How to address an invitation/envelope

The rule is always the same—first the rank, followed by the person's name and surname.

> The 1st Secretary of the Embassy of (country)
> Mr. Michael Jones

Or

> H.E. the Ambassador of (country)
> Mrs. Michael Jones

When the wife is also inviting or invited, write "Mrs." and the husband's name and surname.

> The 1ˢᵗ Secretary of the Embassy of (country)
> and Mrs. Michael Jones

If the wife carries a different surname, write his name and surname as well as hers.

> The 1ˢᵗ Secretary of the Embassy of (country)
> Mr. Michael Jones and Ms. Anne Thompson

When the officer is a woman and the husband is also inviting or invited, write her name and surname and his as well, even if she carries the husband's surname.

> The 1st Secretary of the Embassy of (country)
> Mrs. Isabelle Dupont and Mr. Antoine Dupont

Invitation cards should always be personalized and have the rank, name and surname of the invited guest, type of event, date and time handwritten in black or blue ink. Make sure rank and name are spelled correctly and are accurate, as it gives the wrong impression or may cause some misinterpretations, particularly coming from an embassy, if there is an error.

When sending the invitation card as a reminder, cross out the R.S.V.P. and handwrite p.m. that means *pour mémoire*—to remind

The text may vary between "request(s) the pleasure of your company" or "request(s) the pleasure of the company of . . ."

With today's technology, it is easy and acceptable to have the card personalized and printed in full as shown next.

The Minister-Counselor of the Embassy of (country)
Ms. Paula Smith
requests the pleasure of the company of

Mr. Adrian Banica and Ms. Josy Svteza
at dinner
on Friday, January 4ᵗʰ, at 7.30 pm

Address   *p.m.*
City   *Tel: 000000000*

Examples of text for invitation cards in foreign languages

<u>French</u>

(coat of arms)

Le Conseiller de l'Ambassade de (country)
M. Peter Brown
et Mme Isobel Harris
prient *(rank and name of guest)*

_____

de leur faire l'honneur *(mention type of event)*
le *(date)*   à *(time)*   heures.

Address of event location   R.S.V.P.
City   (Phone number for reply)

Italic—handwritten

Spanish

> (coat of arms)
>
> El Embajador de (country)
> et la Señora de Daniel Smith
> tiene le gusto de invitar a
>
> *(rank and name of guest)* _____
>
> _____
>
> a *(mention type of event)* _____
> el dia *(date)* _____ a las *(time)* _____ horas.
>
> (Address of event location)   S.R.C.
> (City)   (Phone number for reply)

Italic—handwritten

Portuguese

> (coat of arms)
>
> O Primeiro Secretário da Embaixada de (country)
> Sr. John Adams e
> Sr.ª D. Mary Stewart
> têm o prazer de convidar
>
> *(rank and name of guest)* _____
> para *(mention type of event)* _____
>   no dia *(date)* às *(time)* horas.
>
> (Address of event location)   R.S.F.F.
> (City)   (Phone number for reply)

Italic—handwritten

R.S.V.P.: please answer

R.S.V.P. (*Répondez s'il vous plaît*) translates as "respond if you please" (whether you will or will not attend). If a spouse, partner, or any other family member is not specifically mentioned on the invitation card, this means that he or she is not invited and it is inappropriate for them to show up for the event. For widely attended events, the formula "Regrets only" may be used in the invitation, meaning you only respond if not attending.

Respecting the answering procedure is a sign of good manners and a major help for the organizing committee, though in some countries a positive answer doesn't always mean that people will attend the function and/or they may show up with friends and family, causing havoc for the hosting party.

In honor of . . . /To bid farewell

It is a common procedure among diplomats to host lunches or dinners with the single purpose of saying goodbye to a fellow diplomat, working colleague, head of mission, or local official. Settle on a suitable date with the guest of honor and ask him or her for a guest list of people they would like you to invite. In case he or she leaves this up to you as the host, make sure to include his or her acquaintances and also invite people that you know the guest of honor would like to spend time with.

Type the words "To bid farewell to (rank and name of honored guest)" (EN); *"Pour dire au revoir* à . . ." (FR); "*A despedir* a . . ." (SP); "*Para despedir a* . . ." (PT) on a strip of paper and glue it or staple it on the left hand corner of every invitation card as shown on the image below and send one to every guest as a reminder. The guest of honor receives a "normal" invitation card without the strip of paper.

to bid farewell to the 1st Secretary of the Embassy of (country), Mr(s). (Name and surname)

The Consul General of (country)
Ms. Arianne Dupont
requests the pleasure of the company of

_____

_____

at _____

on _____ at _____

Address   R.S.V.P.
City   *Tel: 0000000000*

On this occasion, the guest of honor usually offers the host and hostess a gift from his or her country as a gesture of thanks. This is typically something like a book, a national drink or food item, or a piece of arts and crafts. During lunch or dinner, the host will say a few words relative to the person being honored. This is followed immediately by words from the guest of honor who, among other things, will thank the hosts for the specially arranged meal and acknowledge the presence of everybody else.

In most cases and on behalf of the diplomatic corps, the dean will host a farewell event and offer the departing diplomat a gift offered by all members.

Honoring a person who is either visiting the country (such as a politician, university professor, well-known artist, etc.) or, for example, someone who has been awarded a prize, is a fine gesture and also common in the diplomatic environment. Proceed the same way as mentioned above and write "In honor of . . . (EN); "*À l'honneur de . . .*" (FR); "*Em honra de . . .*" (PT); "*A le honor de . . ."* (SP), on cards sent as reminders to guests, but send the honored guest a card without the strip.

Important note: No guest should ever leave before the guest of honor.

Leaving the country

Hosting one's own farewell cocktail, dinner, or lunch is a nice way to say goodbye to all friends and acquaintances and thank them for time spent together and cooperation at work. Continuing in the same way, write "To bid farewell" (EN); *"Pour dire au revoir"* (FR); *"A despedirse"* (SP), *"Para despedir-se"* (PT) on the paper strip attached to the invitation.

Entertaining

Planning a menu

Entertaining is a very important part of diplomatic life and organizing a meal requires good planning. Of course, practice makes perfect, but creating a routine checklist and shopping list results in fewer mistakes and useless running around and keeps things under control. Provide a good team of professional waiters and always keep an eye on service, but if something goes wrong, don't make a fuss about it in front of guests.

Food is a very important part of any event planning and composing a menu requires the right combination of many different items. The location may be wonderful and the flower arrangements fabulous, but if food and beverage is not adequate, it is all people will remember.

Generally, a meal is composed of three courses: starter, main course, dessert. Sometimes there is cheese before dessert. Salad may or may not be served, but the timing of when it is served differs enormously. In some countries, it is customary to serve it with the main course on a separate side dish, while others like to serve it before or even after the main course. It is best to follow one's own tradition.

While planning the perfect menu consider the following:

- **Color**—Color adds excitement as well as the needed nutrition. Use some flare and use locally produced and in-season vegetables as they taste better and are more affordable.
- **Temperature**—Vary this throughout the meal, serving foods at different temperatures; for example, serve

a cold soup, a hot main course and a dessert at room temperature.

- **Texture**—Crisp, crunchy, smooth, and tender are some of the textures you can use during the meal.
- **Repetitions**—Vary the food group for every course. For example, don't serve lobster soup followed by prawns for the main course.

Knowing your guests preferences and/or food allergies is crucial when choosing food suitable to all tastes, eating habits, and religions. Use previously tested recipes to avoid last-minute disasters. It is always wise to have some replacement food prepared in case one of the guests has some food allergy you were not aware of. The different courses have to combine with each other according to above mentioned rules and still meet with the following requirements:

- **Special needs**—Find out if any guest has a food allergy or any other restriction so that appropriate recipes may be selected and adapted if necessary. (See the table: Religions and food restrictions). No one likes to feel singled out and although ingredients may be differently prepared, dishes should be visually alike without anyone being aware of the difference.
- **For whom and how many guests?**—Generally speaking, men eat more than women. When hosting foreigners, avoid serving very typical foods, and when entertaining nationals, add a local touch by serving a local dish. A large number of guests translates into bigger quantities, meaning more money to buy food and drinks.
- **Formal or informal**—Formal meals require more elaborate food and top-quality ingredients, such as beef filet and lobster, and a professional team of waiters, thereby being more expensive.

- **Lunch vs. dinner**—Lunches are lighter than dinners and less formal and they may also be used as working meetings.
- **Dinnerware**—Do you have the required number of crockery and cutlery for the planned recipes? Dessert fork, knife and dessert plate are sometimes used for starters too.
- **Cold storage and cooking facilities**—Avoid too many oven dishes such as soufflé as a starter, a roast as main course and baked dessert. In hot-weather countries, consider the refrigeration capacity of the kitchen.
- **Budget**—Choose recipes within the budget rather than opting for lower-quality ingredients. For example, if making a chocolate dessert, make sure to use good-quality chocolate; otherwise, prepare a lemon mousse instead.

Religions and food restrictions

	Hindus	Jews	Muslims	Christians
Eggs	some don't eat	yes	yes	yes
Dairy products	some don't eat	yes	yes	yes
Cheese	no	kosher white cheese	halaal white cheese	yes
Fowl	some don't eat	only kosher	only halaal	yes
Lamb	no	only kosher	only halaal	yes
Beef	no	only kosher	only halaal	yes
Pork	no	no	no	yes
Fish	only with fin and scales	only with fin and scales	only with fin and scales	yes
Shellfish	some don't eat	no	some don't eat	yes
Lard	no	no	only halaal	yes
Margarine	some don't eat	only kosher	only halaal	yes
Alcoholic beverages	majority doesn't	only kosher	no	yes
Tea/coffee	yes	yes	yes	yes
Nuts, etc.	yes	yes	yes	yes
Fruits	yes	yes	yes	yes
Fasting	some do	Yom Kippur	Ramadan	some do

Read cookbooks, family recipes, and Internet sites and choose wisely, bearing in mind that courses should complement each other. In countries with poor or deficient supply, always have a fallback plan and a second choice of recipes in mind. The secret to good food is moisture. If you decide to serve a medium-rare filet mignon with a light sauce, add moist potatoes, pasta, etc., and seasonal moist vegetables, such as a succotash, vegetable soufflé, zucchini, crisp green beans, or carrots. Start simple and develop flavors through the meal, applying the same rule when it comes to choosing wine. Avoid foods that are difficult to eat, such as those with bones or shells, very spicy and hot dishes, very sweet desserts, fruit with seeds or stones, and cheese that stretches, like mozzarella on pizzas. Squid, octopus, liver, kidney, or other typical foods can be an acquired taste and may not please guests from different cultures, although it is important to give a national flavor to the meal.

Choosing wine

Diplomatic meals are a perfect opportunity for the host to present and serve national foods and, in wine-producing countries, to serve a selection of their own produce, mainly when entertaining foreign guests. The age-old rule of serving white wine with fish or red wine with meat no longer applies. In fact, it is more important that wines should complement the food being served. For example, grilled fresh tuna may be served with rosé wine in the same way that white meat goes very well with a full-bodied dry white wine. Develop tastes and flavors, as well as wines served, as the meal progresses, starting with lighter dry wines, i.e. dry white wine or rosé followed by red wine. You may also present both white or rosé and red and allow guests to choose.

In the summer or in hot-weather countries, people tend to prefer white and rosé wines to red, which is a more pleasant drink on a cold winter's day. Champagne or sparkling wines may be served before the meal as an aperitif or with dessert for a special toast or celebration.

Store the wine bottles horizontally in a dark cool, dry place. Two days before the event, bring the bottles to the kitchen or pantry. Calculate one bottle per every four guests. Remove the cork one hour before serving, allowing the wine to breathe and enhance the aromas. White wines generally do not require opening so far in advance, but it is important to serve them well chilled. Serve the wine from the bottle with the label facing the guest. Old and rare wines may have some deposit at the bottom; in which case, use a decanter and allow the wine to breathe for two hours.

Recommended temperatures for serving wine:

Champagne or sparkling wine—6ºC (42ºF) to 8ºC (46ºF)
Dry white and rosé—9ºC (48ºF) to 11ºC (53ºF)
Fully bodied dry white wine—10ºC (50ºF) to 12ºC (54ºF)
Red wine—13ºC (55ºF) to 15ºC (59ºF)
Fully bodied red wine—16ºC (61ºF) to 18ºC (66ºF)

Glassware

There are many different kinds, sizes, and shapes of glassware. Using the proper glass enhances the flavor of the drink and helps to keep the temperature correct.

Always handle the glass by the stem or base.

1. Wine glass—Used for wine.
2. Champagne flute—For champagne or sparkling wine.
3. Martini glass—Also known as a "cocktail glass"; used for chilled drinks without ice.
4. Old fashioned glass—Also called a "rocks glass"; used for drinks on the rocks (whisky, *caipirinha*, water).
5. Long drink or Collins glass—Used for soft drinks, juices, and many mixed drinks with or without ice (fruit juice, Coke, beer)
6. Cognac and brandy snifter—For brandy or cognac. Hold by the stem with your middle and ring finger, allowing the hand to warm the drink while holding it.
7. Cordial glass—Used to serve small amounts of port or any liquor.
8. Shot glass—Used for shots or frozen drinks, such as vodka.

Meals

Breakfast

Served between eight and ten, breakfast is often used as a working session among busy professionals and often in hotels.

Breakfast is a very personal meal and most people prefer to eat what they grew up eating. It is a meal that varies enormously from culture to culture and from country to country, making it the most difficult meal to serve to please all tastes. For example, in China breakfast often consists of rice complemented by small amounts of vegetables, meat or fish. A typical breakfast in Egypt and Tunisia will have coffee or tea and a bread accompanied by fish, beans, or falafel. In Mexico, a breakfast burrito, taco, or tostada spiced with salsa is very common and in Germany it is normal to serve cold meats and cheeses and/or sweet toppings like jam, marmalade, and honey with different breads.

If hosting different nationalities together, a buffet breakfast might be the right solution, thus allowing every guest to eat what most pleases him or her. Whether served or buffet-style, the variety offered should be rich and diverse.

Invitation
The invitation may be extended by phone, fax, or e-mail and, if accepted, confirmed by sending a reminder invitation card "p.m." (*pour mémoire*).

On guests' arrival
Serve fruit juice and water.

Table setting and service
Breakfasts are not formal meals, and colorful tablecloths/table mats with matching napkins as well as simple centerpieces of country flowers, may be used.

For a buffet breakfast, use a sideboard for crockery: dishes (two different sizes), bowls for cereals/porridge/rice dishes or fruit salad, and teacups and glasses for either juice or water. Serve the hot beverages (coffee, tea, and milk) in thermoses, and use jugs for water and fruit juices. On a separate table display the food platters, and guests will help themselves at their convenience. Prepare the table(s) for guests to sit down and eat, setting each place with a napkin and the necessary cutlery. Arrange for some items such as sugar bowls, cream, butter, sauces to be put on each table, making self-service easier for guests. Waiters may serve the beverages, remove used dishes, and restock the buffet food platters.

For a Western style served breakfast, set each person's place with a teacup, juice and water glasses, fork and knife, bread plate and napkin. Waiters will serve hot and cold beverages and either present food platters for guests to help themselves or serve previously plated food.

Menu
Choose the appropriate food according to your guests' eating habits, but always include some national and typical dishes from your country.

Coffee break

Coffee break is a light meal, served during recess at lengthy meetings, composed of savory and/or sweet snacks along with hot and cold beverages

Invitation
This does not require any invitation, but it should be mentioned on the meeting's agenda.

Table setting and service
Set a buffet table in the hall near the entrance of the meeting room. Include teacups and glasses, hot and cold beverages, and finger food items so guests can help themselves. If there will be any VIPs present, arrange for waiters to serve drinks and snacks.

Brunch

A mixture of English breakfast and a light lunch, brunch is served between eleven and two and is ideal for a relaxed weekend meal.

Invitation
As it is not a formal meal, a simple phone call will be enough. If you want to make it more formal, send the usual written reminder invitation card "p.m."

On guests' arrival
Serve fruit juice, water, and orange juice—champagne cocktail.

Table setting and service
A buffet, including breakfast and lunch items, is a practical option, allowing guests to choose what most pleases them to eat at that time of the day.

Use color and simplicity and set the table as for lunch, adding a teacup on the top right side of each setting. If you opt for a buffet meal, use a sideboard for crockery as explained above (breakfast), and set the table only with a napkin and cutlery.

Food served
Eggs, sausages, grilled tomatoes, smoked salmon and a variety of breads complemented by some quiches, a selection of cheeses, a choice of cold cuts and roast meat, fresh oysters and seafood, and a variety of salads are some suggestions. You may also add some local breakfast foods. Light desserts and fruit are also welcome. Light dry white and red wines, as well as champagne, tea and coffee, are recommended.

Lunch

Always less formal than dinner, lunch is served between noon and three, depending on local habits and is very often used as a working gathering by professionals.

Invitation
May be done by phone, fax, or e-mail and, if accepted, confirmed by sending a reminder invitation card "p.m."

On guests' arrival
Serve alcoholic and nonalcoholic drinks, as well as some hot and cold snacks. The welcome drink, such as champagne/sparkling wine or port, is offered to everybody. This may be a practical solution, especially if you don't have the capacity to prepare a different drink for each guest.

Table setting and service
Depending on the level of formality of the event, take into account the time of the year and decorate the table accordingly. The hot season is usually more relaxed and strong colors apply. Table linens, serving set, room colors and chosen flowers should coordinate.

In case you don't have any extra help, prepare a meal that does not require last-minute cooking. For example, choose a starter that can be eaten at room temperature and have it on the table before guests sit down. The main course may be served on a sideboard and dessert passed around. It is preferable to serve coffee and tea in a different room.

Food served
Use this opportunity to offer lighter food, such as a vegetarian meal, salads and fruit instead of sweets. Wines have to complement the menu, so dry white and/or rosé wine are suggested, if possible.

Tea or coffee morning

Whether at home or at a tea house, this is a nice option for entertaining women friends. Coffee mornings are held between ten and twelve thirty and tea parties between three and five, preferably during daylight hours.

Invitation
Coffee mornings are informal gatherings and it is normal to invite guests by e-mail or phone call only. For formal tea parties, send a reminder invitation card.

On guests' arrival
Serve fruit juice and water.

Table setting and service
Coffee mornings are always served as a buffet. Use a sideboard for plates, cutlery, teacups and glasses for either juice or water, providing the hot beverages (coffee, tea, and milk) in thermoses, and water and fruit juices in glass jugs. Display the food on the table and guests will help themselves at their leisure. Waiters may serve beverages, remove used dishes and restock the food platters for the buffet.

Tea parties are more formal. Although food is served from a buffet table, tables for guests should be provided.

Food served
Adapt the choice of food to the season and serve things like hot chocolate and warm cakes in winter and fresh fruit juices with fresh vegetable mini sandwiches in the summer. Petit fours, mini pastries, cakes, or sweet pies are always a treat any time of the year.

Bridge, Canasta, or any other game-playing session

A good intellectual exercise, Bridge still remains a popular activity. A game-playing session usually lasts for three hours and depending on the country's habits and time of the year, there are several options:

Morning—Between the first and second session, have a break and present a buffet table with sweet and savory food like mini sandwiches, different pastries, cakes, tea and coffee, but also invite guests for a light lunch at the end.

Afternoon—Serve some snacks in between sessions and an enriched tea or light dinner at the end.

Evening—Serve a light dinner before starting and have a buffet table with cheeses, different breads and mini pastries for a later snack.

Invitation
Choose guests who know how to play the desired game and invite people with the same level of knowledge. Make phone calls to get an answer as soon as possible so that you can make up full tables, where everyone has a partner.

On guests' arrival
For a morning session, serve coffee, tea, juice, or water. In the evening, alcoholic and nonalcoholic drinks are most commonly served.

Table setting and service
Follow the instructions according to the meal you choose to serve.

Food served
Choose the type of food that best suits the meal served.

Cocktail/reception

Ideal for hosting a large group of guests, the cocktail or reception is used for special occasions such as National Day celebrations; after a concert, an artistic show, or art exhibition related to your country; or your own farewell party. It is usually hosted between six and nine, varying according to local traditions. If celebrated at lunchtime, this event is meant for professionals only (stag).

Invitation
Send a written invitation card with RSVP or Regrets only and await the responses.

On guests' arrival
For special occasions such as National Day celebrations or the visit of a head of state, both host and hostess, as well as some officers from the embassy or mission, should form a receiving line, in order of precedence, near the entrance to greet guests.

Table setting and service
Allow for space so that guests can circulate and move around easily. If necessary, remove most of the furniture. Set a bar table and have waiters walking around serving food and drinks and/or have some laid buffet tables. Decorate with flowers and remove small decorative items, just in case of breakage or theft.

Food served
There are basically two different ways to serve cocktails: bite-sized canapés (hot and cold) being served by waiters, or a buffet meal. Guests have to eat while standing, so the food being served should not contain any shells or bones and should be bite size.

Checklist

Date and time of event:_____
Number of guests: _____
Estimated budget: _____

Invitation list
- ❏ Gather names and addresses for guest list
- ❏ Compose guest list
- ❏ Create layout and print invitation cards and envelopes
- ❏ Mail invitation cards
- ❏ Arrange for special delivered invitations
- ❏ Note responses

Requirements for the reception site
- ❏ Easy access location
- ❏ Parking area
- ❏ Security level
- ❏ Indoors or outdoors option
- ❏ Verification of rooms to be used and access ways (elevators, stairs, handicap ramps)
- ❏ Lounges or other private rooms
- ❏ Tent, umbrellas, or any other form of shade
- ❏ Lighting system (outdoors and indoors); need for extra generator
- ❏ Kitchen and pantry facilities
- ❏ Easy access to toilets
- ❏ Cooling/heating system
- ❏ Coat check (necessary on cold or rainy days)

At event location
- ❏ Antimosquitoes—incense, citronella, etc.
- ❏ Ashtrays (outdoor)
- ❏ Coat clerk

- ☐ Security personnel
- ☐ Site decoration (flower arrangements, candles)
- ☐ Table and chairs (if applicable)
- ☐ Tablecloths, napkins
- ☐ WCs cleaning and maintenance personnel
- ☐ WCs supplies (soap, toilet paper, paper towels, garbage containers and bags, tissues, hand cream)

Service, food, and beverages
- ☐ Bar tables, tablecloth, bottle openers, wine glasses, and others
- ☐ Beverages—alcoholic and nonalcoholic, ice and refrigeration capacity
- ☐ Crockery and cutlery for guests, serving glasses, bottle openers, serving trays, serving plates, serving cutlery, etc.
- ☐ Food (canapés—hot and cold, savory and sweet) and/or buffet meal
- ☐ Garbage containers and bags
- ☐ Reception desk and chairs
- ☐ Reception personnel
- ☐ Waiters, cooks, and barmen

Entertainment
- ☐ Anthems (national and host country)
- ☐ Flags (national and host country) and others
- ☐ Microphone and sound system
- ☐ Music—background (taped); live players
- ☐ Stage

Dinner

Served between seven and nine, dinner is the most formal meal of the day.

Invitation
The invitation may be done by phone, fax, or e-mail and if accepted is confirmed with a reminder invitation card "p.m." (*pour mémoire*). For very formal occasions, send a R.S.V.P. invitation card six weeks in advance and wait for the response.

On guests' arrival
Serve alcoholic and nonalcoholic drinks as well as some hot and cold snacks. The welcome drink is the same drink for everybody, such as champagne/sparkling wine or port and it may be more convenient to serve, especially if you don't have the capacity to prepare a different drink for each guest.

Seating options
With the exception of state dinners where protocol is strict, there are several possible options for dinner. Depending on the level of formality, number of guests, availability of waiters and style of service, here are some options:

- **Seated and served dinner at single table**—This is the most formal form of entertaining.
  Pros: Besides always being a beautiful setting, guests can communicate easily with each other (if the table is not too long).
  Cons: For more than six people, a seating plan and a good team of professional waiters are required. Inform waiters beforehand of the service precedence at the table, bearing in mind that ladies are served before men.

- **Seated and served dinner using different tables**—This is used if the number of guests cannot fit at a single table and is also a formal way of entertaining.
  Pros: Hosts sit separately, therefore generating different presidencies and consequently creating two more

"important" seats. This format is easier to rearrange in case some guests do not show up.

Cons: Requires more space, more waiters and more centerpieces or other decoration elements, as well as a seating plan.

For big events it is advisable to give each table a themed name, mentioning it on the seating plan or giving each guest a card with their seat location.

- **Buffet**—This is less formal than any of the above mentioned situations. It is very practical for bigger groups and when the exact number of guests is not known. If possible, provide tables where guests can sit informally and eat.

  Pros: It does not require any seating arrangement, uses fewer waiters and guests interact more.

  Cons: Provide for one serving food station for every thirty guests. It requires more quantity and a wider choice of food, always without bones or shells, that may be eaten easily with only a fork.

The buffet table should display the foods in the correct order to be eaten: the cold plates on one side followed by the hot plates. Dessert and cheeses should be brought in afterward or set on a separate table. Prepare one food table for every thirty to forty guests to avoid long lines.

Service

For a seated, served dinner, food may either be presented on serving platters from which guests may help themselves (*à la française*) or already plated. Both options require a good team of professional waiters. Only use the first option if you know guests are at ease with this type of service; otherwise, opt for plated food. Before the meal, inform waiters of precedence at the table, or draw a plan and hang it on the wall or door leading to the dining room.

The proper way of serving is "left in, right out." Empty dishes, plated food, food platters, side dishes and bread (solids) are presented from the left and drinks (liquids) from the right side of the guest. Once all guests are done eating, plates are taken from the right. Nothing should ever be passed in front of any guest.

Tea, coffee and after-dinner drinks are better served in a different area, permitting guests to interact and move around.

Serving yourself
When the food platter is presented to you (from the left), hold the serving spoon with your right hand, the serving fork with your left hand and help yourself. Pay attention, avoid spills and don't be choosy. Put the food gently on your plate and when finished position the fork on top of the spoon and place them on the outer edge of the serving platter, ready for the next guest to handle.

Checklist

Three weeks before
- ❏ Draw up a guest list
- ❏ Set the date
- ❏ Invite guests
  - • Make phone call
  - • Inquire about food allergies or restrictions
  - • Send written invitation card—p.m.
- ❏ Set budget
- ❏ Plan menu, appetizers, and beverages
  - • Select recipes for starter, main course, and dessert, and choose wines accordingly
  - • Make shopping list

- Determine service at table—*à la française*, plated, or buffet
- ❏ Choose and reserve location (when applicable)
- ❏ Hire extra staff (waiters, cook)

Two weeks before
- ❏ Cook and freeze dishes/foods
- ❏ Hire waiters, barmen, cook (optional)
- ❏ Order prepared food

One week before
- ❏ Order flower arrangements
- ❏ Polish silverware
- ❏ Print menu cards (optional)
- ❏ Select table linens (tablecloth, table mats, cloth napkins, tray mats, cocktail napkins)
- ❏ Select tableware, glassware, cutlery, serving jars, bar glassware, ice bucket, trays

Two to three days before
- ❏ Buy or start making ice cubes
- ❏ Confirm help
- ❏ Shop for food and beverage

One day before
- ❏ Check coat closet (when applicable)
- ❏ Check social WC (hand towels, soap, toilet paper, etc.)
- ❏ Do seating arrangement (placement) and write name cards
- ❏ Put drinks in fridge
- ❏ Prepare food (sweet and savory)
- ❏ Select background music

On the day
- ❏ Buy bread
- ❏ Collect flower arrangements or buy flowers
- ❏ Cooking final touches

❏ Prepare appetizers
❏ Select drinks for before and after the meal

Three hours before
❏ Explain procedure to hired waiters
❏ Set the table
❏ Place name cards on the table according to seating arrangement
❏ Display seating plan
❏ Prepare ice for serving
❏ Prepare tray for drinks after meal
❏ Prepare tray with coffee and tea cups
❏ Plate appetizers
❏ Finish cooking

One hour before
❏ *Relax* for thirty minutes
❏ Get ready to receive guests

Fifteen minutes before
❏ Light candles and turn on lights of social area (if applicable)
❏ Fill water glasses (dining table)
❏ Serve bread on bread plates (dining table)
❏ Play background music
❏ Have receiving party in place (when applicable)

Zero minutes
❏ Welcome your guests
❏ Make necessary introductions
❏ Serve appetizers and drinks
❏ Converse with every guest

Thirty minutes into the event
❏ Invite guests to table and start the meal
❏ Proceed with the meal

After the meal
- ❐ Serve tea and/or coffee
- ❐ Serve chocolates or treats
- ❐ Serve after-dinner drinks
- ❐ Serve water

Number of waiters needed

The amount of waiters needed for an event depends on their proficiency, the number of guests, the type of function and the country's costumes and habits. As a guide:

Formal seated dinner	one waiter serving food for every six guests
	one waiter serving drinks for every ten guests
Buffet	one waiter to remove used plates and glasses for every ten guests
	one waiter to serve drinks for every twenty guests
Reception/cocktail	one waiter serving finger food for every thirty guests
	one waiter serving drinks for every thirty guests

Setting the Table

Based on the level of formality of the event, decide what best suits your table setting: either a white linen tablecloth and white cloth napkins for formal events or white or colored table mats for less formal meals. At the official residence, use the official dinning service, silver cutlery, and stem glassware when so required. In either case, use a felt cloth underneath to avoid noises and keep the mat from slipping. If you want to introduce a touch of class, use a charger or *sous-plat* with a round cloth doily over it and put the plate on top. The charger may be left on the table throughout the meal or removed before serving dessert.

Make sure every item to be used is clean and without any fingerprints.

Set each place setting forty-five centimeters (seventeen inches) apart, with the service plate in the middle (with or without a charger). Lay the cutlery necessary for the chosen menu and remember that soup spoons and knives are on the right of the plate and forks are on the left (with the exception of the oyster fork, which would be on the right side). Knives will always be placed with the blade facing inward. Align all the lower edges of the pieces of cutlery that are at the sides and put them three centimeters (one and a half inches) higher than the bottom rim of the plate (or charger) and three centimeters (one and a half inches) away from it. The dessert cutlery is placed horizontally, at the top of the place setting, with the spoon handle facing right and fork handle facing left. In some countries, the dessert cutlery may be set alongside the main course cutlery, closest to the eating plate. Finger bowls are only presented and placed on the top left side of the eating plate and used after having eaten food with your hands, such as shellfish or fruit, never served at official dinners.

The place setting

If you can navigate the place setting, you'll never unknowingly steal your neighbor's bread or napkin again.

The **glasses** are placed on the top right-hand side above the meat knife. From left to right, the order is: water, red wine and white wine (or rosé) and then champagne, liqueur, or port glasses are put behind the wine glasses. **Napkins** may be folded in fantastic shapes and put on the main plate or simply folded in a rectangular or square shape and placed on the left side after the cutlery. The **bread plate** is placed on the top left-hand side, the butter knife on it with the blade facing inward. If using a **side dish**, placed it on the left as close as possible to the serving plate or charger.

Coffee and tea are generally served in a different room, but in the case of a working dinner meeting, after removing the charger and/or used plate, place the cup in the middle of the setting with the handle in the four o'clock position and the spoon on the right on the saucer.

Butter holders and elegant **salt and pepper** containers or shakers may be on the table and if necessary passed around. **Ashtrays** are no longer used during dinner time. For decoration, use flowers matching the formality and colors of the dining room, although fruit or any other items can create very interesting and beautiful centerpieces. Just make sure they are not so tall that guests can't see over them. **Candles** are also a nice decorative element but should be odorless.

Some notes:

- Never lay a setting without a serving plate (empty or not), even if using a charger.
- If using a bowl or a different-shaped glass, for example, for soup, shrimp cocktail, or ice cream, always use a plate under it. When finished eating, guests should place the used utensil on that plate.
- Food is never put in direct contact with the charger.

Examples of menus and respective table settings

Fish, meat, dessert.
Water, red wine, white wine.

Soup, fish, meat, dessert.
Water, red wine, white wine, champagne and port.

Soup, starter, fish, dessert.
Water, red or white wine.

Starter, fish, meat, dessert.
Water, red wine, white wine, champagne and port.

Nowadays it is fashionable to drink red wine from bigger goblets, but the order of setting the glasses remains the same: from left to right water, red wine, white wine.

Starter, meat, dessert.
Water, red wine.

Arrangement of Seating

The arrangement of seating is a very sensitive and important issue in the diplomatic world and should be done in advance. Seats are attributed according to the host's country's protocol rules of precedence. It is not an easy task and solutions have to be subtle so as not to offend anyone. Situations rarely repeat themselves and in spite of the various options, there will always be questions. Learn how to bend the rules here and there and be prepared to use a great dose of common sense. It is often said that when in doubt, give the most intelligent person a lower-ranked seat because he or she will understand. If one or more guests don't show up, remove the seat altogether and redo the seating plan.

In most countries, the seat on the right-hand side of the male host is the most important one for a lady, followed by the seat on the host's left. The same applies for a male guest, referring to the hostess's right and left sides. Ideally men and women should be seated alternately around the table.

Procedure

When assigning a person's seat, several factors have to be taken into account:

- Host(s)—First determine where host and hostess sit: at the top of the table or across from one another at the centre of the table. In the case where there is no hostess, the presidency of the table should be shared with somebody of the opposite sex, such as the guest of honor (if there is one) or the highest-ranking guest or his/her spouse. For a meal with professionals only, the presidency is shared with the highest-ranking guest.

- Rank—When guests have the same profession (diplomats, for example), follow the career hierarchy: Ambassador, Ministers, Chargé d'Affaires a.e., Chargé d' Affaires a.i., Minister-Counselors, Counselors, First Secretaries, Second Secretaries, Third Secretaries and Assistant Attachés. Seat them accordingly.

- Seniority—When guests share the same profession *and* rank, the one who has occupied that position longest has precedence over the others. For example, Johan Klaus, the First Secretary of Embassy X, assumed his posting in March 2008 and so has precedence over Katri Mayl, the First Secretary of Embassy Y, who assumed functions in January 2011.

- Public vs. private sector—Check your country's rules of protocol and then seat accordingly.

- Age and sex—In cases where the guests are not professionals, older ladies precede over younger men.

- Special guests—A female guest of honor sits on the male host's right and a male guest of honor on the hostess's right side or shares the presidency if there is no cohost.

- Spouses—Assume their spouse's professional rank and position and do not sit them next to each other, or if there is more than one table, sit them at separate tables.

Name cards

When hosting more than six people, it is advisable to use name cards with the guest's rank and/or job title and name mentioned. Place them at the top of the place setting; you may print an individual menu card as well.

H. E. the Ambassador of Sweden
Mrs. Marta Svensson

Use a table plan (placement) or any other graphic form of letting your guests know where to sit and display it at the entrance of the dining room.

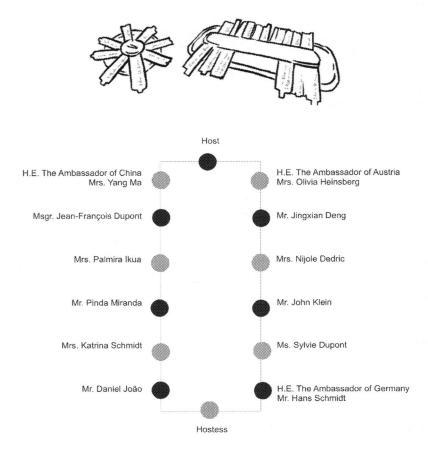

Host

H.E. The Ambassador of China Mrs. Yang Ma	H.E. The Ambassador of Austria Mrs. Olivia Heinsberg
Msgr. Jean-François Dupont	Mr. Jingxian Deng
Mrs. Palmira Ikua	Mrs. Nijole Dedric
Mr. Pinda Miranda	Mr. John Klein
Mrs. Katrina Schmidt	Ms. Sylvie Dupont
Mr. Daniel João	H.E. The Ambassador of Germany Mr. Hans Schmidt

Hostess

Table Manners

Being invited for a meal is a very frequent and important event in diplomatic life and table manners play an important part in creating a favorable impression. Though diplomats tend to use European table manners and table setting, dining etiquette rules vary greatly around the world and may be different from what you are used to. Having good table manners shows proper education and respect toward guests and oneself. Once you are invited to a national's house for a meal, learn about the local table manners and when in doubt, do as the host or hostess does. Mistakes happen; simply excuse yourself.

Being faced with an array of silverware and glasses at a formal dinner can be daunting. Knowing what to use, when and how can be challenging and proper table manners may seem complicated.

Approach the table and sit where told by the host or hostess. Men should help the ladies by pushing in the chair and only sit after the hostess has sat down. These are just some of the basics, but soon after mastering them, you will feel more comfortable and at ease.

With this know-how, you will be able to adapt to any situation, even more sophisticated occasions, naturally and graciously. Always remember to respect different customs, learning about them before hosting people of different nationalities or traveling to a new country.

Posture

Good posture at the table is important. Sit up straight, with both feet flat on the floor. Don't lean back in your chair. While eating, keep your elbows close to your sides and don't try to "fly" with open wings. If you are not eating, keep your hands on your lap (accepted among Anglo-Saxons), or rest your wrists on the edge of the table. At informal gatherings, or among friends, sometimes it's acceptable for you to put your elbows on the table while talking and between courses, but never at formal or official dinners. Your forearm should never be on the table.

Always

Sometimes

Never

Don't leave the table until indicated to do so, and once the meal is over, stand up only after the hostess or the host (in her absence) has done so. In case of emergency, like a sudden attack of coughing or sneezing, try to signal the hostess before leaving the table, leaving the napkin on your chair. On your return, excuse yourself discretely and sit quietly. If someone else is choking seriously, help immediately.

If you spill a glass of wine or some food flies off your plate, act naturally, remembering that we are all humans and accidents happen. Guests and hosts should never make a big fuss when something like that happens.

Starting to eat

Firstly, find the napkin and open it and place it on your lap. Never tuck it into your collar. If you think it might slip, discreetly try to tuck it into your waistband. If it falls on the floor, pick it up or allow the male guest sitting next to you to do so and place it back on the lap. Use the cutlery from the outside in and in the reverse order of the food served.

Wait until everyone is served and start eating each course after the hostess or, in her absence, the host has done so. If soup is the first course, hold the spoon in your right hand and place your other wrist on the edge of the table. Bring the spoon toward your mouth, always keeping your back straight. When finished, leave the spoon in the soup plate or on the plate below, if served in a bowl or different container.

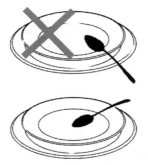

When eating eggs, salad, or any pasta dish, only use the fork, keeping your hand as explained before. For the main course, usually either fish or meat, use both knife and fork at the same time, with the handles resting in the palms of your hand. Proceed to cut the food and eat it.

When engaging in any conversation, rest your cutlery in a crossed position over the plate. Do not overload the fork and eat slowly without making any noises. Once you have finished, leave both knife and fork parallel on the plate at a 4:20 position.

When served the same course a second time, you may start eating right away and do not have to wait until everybody has been served again.

Hold the glass by the stem and put it back in the same position, always wiping your mouth before and after drinking. If you don't drink wine, politely refuse when being served. Never cover the glass with your hand or tip it upside down, or you may cause a spill. During a toast, accept some wine and pretend to sip some at toasting time even if you do not drink wine.

If eating bread, tear off a piece with your hands downward so as not to spread the breadcrumbs all over your neighboring guest, then eat it. You may butter it or use any kind of spread available, using the meat knife if there is no butter knife.

Consommé or bouillon may be served in an appropriate two-handle cup and eaten with a spoon or, depending on its thickness, can be sipped, even if a spoon is provided. Hold both handles and drink it slowly without slurping. If using the spoon, place it on the plate below when finished, not inside the cup.

Guests should taste the food before seasoning it. Sauces like applesauce, mustard, or horseradish are usually placed on the side of the food plate and food is dipped in. When asked to pass the salt, pass both salt and pepper, even though only one was requested. Pass the bread basket on if it is close to you, and help yourself last when it comes back.

Eating certain types of foods

At formal meals, it is always better to avoid serving difficult foods such as cheese that stretches or meat or fish with bones or shells, with the exception of fresh oysters. On the other hand, asparagus, artichokes leaves, shelled seafood, grapes and cherries, may be eaten by hand. In such cases, a water bowl should be put on the top left side of the place setting. If in doubt, follow the hostess, or the host in her absence.

When you feel a bone or an olive pip, make a fist with your hand and, as discreetly as possible, spit the particle into your hand and put it on the side of your plate. If some food gets caught between your teeth, try to dislodge it slowly by using the tip of your tongue or some water. Leave the usage of toothpicks for private moments.

Conversing

Create a pleasant atmosphere and talk to the people around you in a soft tone of voice. Avoid hot topics or themes that might offend or leave others in dire straits and don't monopolize the conversation. Enjoy the moment.

At the restaurant

If invited to a restaurant, while choosing from a menu, ask the other guests what they are having and choose a dish within the same price range. If you have any food allergy, ask the waiter not to include that particular ingredient in your dish, but don't "create" a new recipe by asking to change the dish completely. As a rule, the person who invites pays for the meal; therefore, don't insist on paying for it. At the end, if you are paying it is best to settle the account once every guest has left the restaurant.

Tipping varies from country to country and is always better given in cash.

Toasts and speeches

It is a nice gesture to welcome guests with an informal toast at the beginning of the meal and after the wine has been served. The host says some simple welcoming words and raises his or her glass for a toast with every guest doing the same. On more formal occasions, or when the event requires a speech, such as a farewell dinner, the host makes a speech ending with toast at the beginning of the meal or before dessert is served. Guests raise their glasses and toast as well. The guest of honor responds immediately in the same way and guests toast again.

Golden Rules

- **Always** sit down after the hostess or, in her absence, the host and immediately place your napkin on your lap. Use it only to wipe your mouth and never as a rag.
- **Always** start eating after the hostess or, in her absence, the host.
- **Always** use the cutlery from the outside in. After finishing each course, place the used utensils parallel and at the 4:20 position on the plate. While engaging in a long conversation, or if you haven't finished eating yet, place fork and knife on the plate in an inverted V position.
- **Always** maintain an upright posture, keeping your back straight, both loose fists on the table and your feet flat on the ground.
- **Always** chew with your mouth closed.
- **Always** wipe your mouth before and after drinking and be sure to swallow the food before taking a sip.

- **Always** break the bread with your fingers rather than biting it. Butter the broken piece and eat it, but never dip it in sauces or soup.
- **Always** thank your hosts for the meal.

- **Never** play with any table utensils.
- **Never** leave the table during the meal, except in urgent situations, such as intense coughing, sneezing or choking.
- **Never** talk with a full mouth.
- **Never** lick or put your knife in your mouth or point with any utensil.
- **Never** reach over someone's plate for something; instead, ask for the item to be passed.
- **Never** use your fingers to push food onto your spoon or fork.
- **Never** slurp your food or eat noisily.
- **Never** blow your nose on a napkin (serviette).
- **Never** pick food out of your teeth with your fingers.
- **Never** indicate that you notice anything unpleasant in the food. Put it on the side of your plate and continue eating.

The Perfect Host/Hostess

Entertaining is much more than preparing a menu, as many other things have to be considered. The perfect hosts are "professional organizers" who know that details count and make the difference. They wish to please guests and make them feel comfortable throughout the event. Planning is very important and avoids last-minute rushing and stress. When guests start arriving, hosts have to be ready to greet, introduce and entertain, always displaying good manners and acting naturally.

Discretely check the way service is running and avoid getting up every five minutes to give orders or constantly rushing to the kitchen.

Talk to every guest and engage everyone in the conversation. If one of them doesn't speak the language (a situation to be avoided, but it sometimes happens), ask somebody to act as a translator and never leave the guest unattended. People like to talk and express ideas, but when someone is monopolizing the conversation or is being inappropriate, try to change the subject, keeping the atmosphere pleasant and respectful. Social occasions are meant to be enjoyable and important topics should be left for professional meetings.

Hosting an event at home versus a restaurant keeps the gathering private. One can talk about any topic and not worry about eavesdropping. Also, there is no time restraint, food is carefully prepared in a clean environment (important to consider in some parts of the world), and, let's face it, it's cheaper! Generally speaking, hosting an event is always a special occurrence, and an opportunity to get to know people better and create a bond.

Decorate the room with flowers and candles and play some background music while being pleasant and gracious. One good piece of advice is to take thirty minutes prior to the guests' arrival and relax. Remember that minor organizational flaws are only noticed by the organizer.

- On guests' arrival, greet them one by one and introduce them to guests they have never met before.
- Remember every guest's name.
- Keep track of service and see that everybody has a drink and is comfortably seated.
- Provide for snacks and drinks before lunch or dinner.
- Enjoy yourself and make sure every guest is comfortable as well.
- In due time, direct guests to the table and show them their seats (for formal dinners use a table plan).
- Sit properly at the table and observe good table manners.
- Welcome everybody with a simple toast (at the beginning of the meal or before dessert). At more formal occasions (such as farewell dinners), the guest of honor responds in the same form.
- As a host/hostess, be the first to start eating.
- Keep the conversation going and raise topics, if necessary.
- Remain seated throughout the meal, and at the end of the meal, be the first to leave the table.
- When saying goodbye, thank every guest for their attendance and the gift, if applicable.

Dealing with mishaps

If someone calls and excuses him/herself, remove the seat from the table and redo the seating plan.

If one guest is missing and dinner is running late because of their absence, wait for thirty minutes before trying to contact him or her. If unsuccessful, proceed with the meal, leaving his or her seat untouched, in case they arrive. If the person shows up during the meal, serve them the course other guests are having. But if dessert is already being served, bend the rules and serve the main course to them as well.

If somebody spills wine, react normally and say it happens to you all the time. Help to clean up and make your guest feel okay. Remove the broken pieces and replace the glass. Most importantly, don't make the person feel uncomfortable!

If a guest is choking, help the person and stand them up, if necessary. Act naturally without making a big fuss about it.

If guests swap the name cards at the table, ignore it and proceed with the seating plan.

The Perfect Guest

As a rule of thumb, be polite at all times.

- Accept the invitation; otherwise, express thanks and excuse yourself.
- Always inform the hosts of any food allergy or dietary restriction so the menu may be prepared in accordance. Not doing so may cause some distress (it might be difficult to cook something at the last minute) and leaves hosts in dire straits and feeling uncomfortable.
- Be punctual and appropriately dressed for the occasion. If you are delayed or for some reason can't attend the lunch or dinner at the last minute, do whatever you can to call the hosts or anyone else who can let them know.
- Greet other guests, mingle and engage in conversations.
- When calling on someone, consider the hosts' cultural background and take a suitable gift or send flowers the morning of the lunch or dinner (if appropriate). For example, offering a bottle of wine to a Muslim or white flowers to a Japanese lady can be offensive.
- Take your designated seat.
- Start eating only after the hostess or, in her absence, the host begins.
- On departure, always thank the hosts and call the day after as well.
- Under normal circumstances, switch off your mobile phone or use it only if strictly necessary, speaking softly. Avoid constant messaging or e-mail checks.
- Be present and enjoy every moment.

Gifts and procedure

Offering a gift is a nice, appreciated gesture toward the host as a way of saying thank you for the invitation. On the other hand, when attending meetings of any kind, lunches or dinners in honor of somebody, cocktails, or National Day receptions, it is not required to take any gift. For events hosted at restaurants or hotels, it is nice to offer a small token, but flowers are not recommended.

Before purchasing flowers, find out about the local procedure and the person's cultural habits. This is a sensitive topic that varies considerably regarding the species given and whether there is an even or odd number of flowers in the bunch. In countries like Portugal or Spain, for example, it is customary to have flowers delivered the morning of the event, while in Germany flowers are given unwrapped on arrival. Wine is highly appreciated in wine-drinking countries like France and Angola, but not so in Saudi Arabia or for people who, for religious reasons don't drink. Sweets or chocolates are generally well accepted all over the world, as well as arts and crafts.

As hosts, find out about each guest's preference and tradition concerning opening their gift publically. When in doubt, ask before doing so. Don't be offended and respect cultural differences. For example, in Asia and Mexico, gifts are private and should never be opened in public but thanks are expressed upon reception. In the United States, they should be opened and thanks should be given immediately.

If flowers are delivered, use them for decorating the room and thank the donor on arrival. When presented with a bunch of flowers by the guest, have them put in a vase immediately and display them. A bottle of wine or liquor is meant for private consumption at a later time. On the other hand, it is nice to share some of the chocolates and sweets received, at coffee time.

On the Move Again

Nowadays, it is easy to know almost everything about your new posting before you even get there. Just Google it and in a flash, you will learn about the geographical location, weather, population, commercial and political data, or any other general information you may want. For more detailed information, it is best to contact people you know who have previously been posted there, read post reports and ask as many questions as you think relevant.

It is a nice gesture to write or e-mail your new Head of Mission. Show appreciation for the nomination and express how glad you are to work together in the near future. The wife of the junior officer should also introduce herself to the ambassador's wife both before and upon arrival.

Important information to enquire about

Security
Healthcare facilities, vaccines needed
Advisable living neighborhoods
Education: schools, universities, language classes
Cost of living and other financial matters
Insurance policies: health, house, car, etc.
Good shopping locations (food, clothes, household goods, and electronics)
Special food items to import
International moving companies
Banks and ATMs/cash machines
Pet traveling requirements

Keep an open mind and try to adapt as quickly as possible. Remember that nowhere on Earth is perfect and that every country has some good things about it. Understand that people's perspectives differ. Respect other cultures and learn as much as possible from other people. Being able to speak the local language helps for communicating and shows your interest in the country and its people. Avoid using sign language as, due to cultural differences, what seems innocent in one country may be offensive in another.

There might be times when things don't work the same way as they do at home or you cannot find that particular detergent brand or food item that is so important for that special recipe and you may feel frustrated. This is normal, but you have to be open minded. Try to avoid criticizing and let these things go. They are part of your new experience and there are much more important things in life!

Read about the new country and find out about interesting places to visit. Join local sports clubs or social groups and participate in as many activities as possible, trying to integrate as soon as you can. This will certainly help to make things easier.

Getting ready for the packers

Experience says that if you mentally plan everything first, things will run more smoothly afterward. Most importantly, don't panic; start organizing!

If you are allowed to take your furniture and other personal items with you, sort through them and decide on those things that you really want to take. Use this opportunity to declutter. Children outgrow their clothes very fast and, by the time the container arrives at the new destination, they won't fit anymore. Generally speaking, any clothes you haven't worn in more than two years you probably will never wear again. Remember that food items have a short shelf life. Check the voltage used at the new destination, because it may not be worth taking electric appliances if they cannot work. For things that require more attention, like sound systems, check that there is a local agent for repairs and parts.

Take photographs of each room as well as of all contents inside every cabinet and wardrobe. This is a simple and inexpensive way to remind you of all of your items. Take individual pictures of the more valuable items, such as paintings, furniture, and antique china, and print two sets, taking one with you.

For insurance purposes and your personal organization, make an inventory list. Create some key categories such as Paintings (P), Furniture (F), Kitchen items (K), Antiques (A), Crockery (C) and Miscellaneous (X), and number each important item. Prioritize items using the A-B-C method, i.e. A for essential items and immediate unpacking, B for important contents, and C for things you won't need right away and will open last.

How to fly your cat or dog

Moving from place to place is one characteristic of diplomatic life that takes courage and to which not everybody adapts. As an adult, one learns to see the positive side and enjoy it as part of life's experiences. Children accept changes depending on the way their parents view them. Pets are part of the family, but they don't fully understand what is happening. Before the packers arrive, they feel the buzz and that something is different but are not really sure what. This is something to be conscious of. Be more understanding during packing and on the day of departure.

As soon as you are told of your new destination, find out about all necessary documentation and vaccines or blood tests for your pet for traveling and entering the new country. Requirements vary from country to country and are also affected by the prevalence of diseases at that particular time, so start the process in due time. According to the condition of your animal's health, a tranquilizer may or may not be necessary for the journey, but your vet will be able to advise you.

Have the cage measurements and pet's weight with you when making the flight arrangements, making sure that the cage is in accordance with IATA regulations and adequate for the pet's size (see IATA Live Animal Regulations). Book your flight ahead of time, as not every flight carries live animals. Try to find the shortest and least stressful flight. Keep in mind that, if your pet is not booked on the same flight as you, it must be checked in as cargo at least three hours before departure. Add this time to the flying time, plus another hour at the destination to have your pet released from cargo. Consider all this when thinking about how long your pet will be in the cage and away from you and therefore how much tranquilizer it may need.

Only small dogs and cats may travel in the cabin with you; otherwise, they will travel in the hold in a specially heated and ventilated compartment meant for live animals. However, it is always good to confirm that your pet is actually on board and that the hold is heated.

Take a picture of your pet and have it with you at all times. In the event that the cage is lost or left behind (which can happen), this will help. Write the animal's name, as well as the owner's name, address, and phone contacts at the final destination, on the cage.

Some questions for the airline:

- How far in advance do I (with my pet) have to check in at the airport and exactly where is this done?
- If the flight is rerouted (in case the animal travels alone), will I be informed?

- What is the cost per kilo?
- Which papers should accompany my pet?
- Which papers do I bring to pick up my pet?
- Will my pet check through customs here or upon arrival?

Security

Security is a major concern nowadays, no matter where you are in the world, although some countries are safer than others. Security measures exist to limit the occurrence of terrorist activity, but remember there is little one can do to prevent being caught up in a terrorist attack. At airports, hotels, and places with extra security measures, be patient and thankful, and comply with these measures, which are there for your protection. Criminal and terrorist attacks are planned, but the plans' camouflaging is very often sloppy, leaving traces for early detection. Be aware, because denial can be deadly.

The most prevalent threat you face and over which you can have some control, is crime. Be responsible for your own security at all times and protect your family and surroundings.

When first arriving in a new city, find out where the safest residential areas are before renting a house or apartment. Don't rely only on one realtor's opinion, don't try to be creative or think you can outsmart everybody and follow your colleagues' advice. Diplomats tend to live close together (usually in nice neighborhoods), making it easier to socialize and attend official functions with less driving involved. This is even more true for countries with social or political unrest when the local security forces have to protect the area.

Personal safety

Be alert at all times and pay attention to any unusual events. Make this a habit and report anything unusual. Never go off with strangers or accept things from people who approach you on the street and avoid going to isolated areas alone. Stay away from public demonstrations or overcrowded areas, as they are easy targets for bombs. Know where all family members are at all times, particularly during difficult situations. If any incident occurs, report it to the police and make it known, in full detail, to the diplomatic community.

Children are the most vulnerable. Teach them to say *no* to strangers and to never accept anything from them. Explain how to answer the phone without giving away too much information and to never allow anyone in the house without adult supervision.

Vary daily routines and all predictable patterns, such as jogging at the same hour every day. Different schedules and different routes will disorient burglars or potential kidnappers.

Use only reputable taxi operators and make sure to be the sole passenger. Do not allow the driver to stop and pick up any unknown passenger along the way. In some countries, this is very common. The ride may be more expensive, but it is always better to be safe than sorry! Make sure your luggage is actually inside the vehicle, lock all doors, and don't open your windows. Ask about safety on public transportation before using it.

Do not open suspicious or unexpected mail and don't give your home address to unknown people.

At home

Create emergency plans in case of outside attacks, fires, or invasion. Rehearse these safety drills, always being aware of the best procedures to escape danger and get help. Keep a list of emergency numbers near the phone, as well as mobile and landline numbers of embassy or consulate staff.

In very troubled areas or countries at war, designate an internal room in the house as a safe haven for all family members to hide in. (The bathroom is a good option because it has water and a toilet!) Furnish this room with supplies: a landline phone, fresh water, long-life or tinned food, flashlight, battery-operated radio, extra batteries, first aid kit and personal items such as clothes, blankets, and toys.

Use both silent and audible alarm systems. It can take as long as ten to twenty minutes for the alarm company or police to show up after an alarm has been tripped. Install smoke and fire detectors and have some fire extinguishers on all floors and in the kitchen.

Have your house lit on the outside and consider putting in light sensors that switch lights on automatically. If you live in an apartment, keep the outside light over the main door on during the dark hours to be able to see before being seen. Keep a spare key at the embassy or consulate or with a colleague. Don't hide it under the carpet or in a flower pot.

Trim any bushes and trees around your home that could become hiding spots for burglars, who may even use overhanging branches to climb onto your roof.

If the sliding doors are not safe, put a dowel down in the door channel before going out so that the door can't be opened wide enough for a person to get through. Before leaving the house, make your home seem occupied by using timers to turn lights, radios and TVs on and off randomly.

Nowadays, burglars troll social media sites looking for targets, so don't post vacation photos or tell of your whereabouts on Facebook while you are away.

Household staff

When hiring help, choose carefully and ask for reliable references, preferably carrying out reference checks in person. It is important to always treat your household staff with respect and when possible pay them fair or even above-average wages.

Advise them on discretion and instruct them on answering the door and phone calls. It's important that they report the presence of strangers in the neighborhood and never tell anyone where you are or when you are expected back. Any serviceperson coming to the house should be accompanied by someone from the household at all times. If you are forced to fire anyone, consider changing the locks.

In the car

Keep the doors locked at all times and the windows up. Leave enough space between your vehicle and the one in front for an emergency escape. If hit from behind, do not exit the car before making sure it's safe. In case of carjacking or any other form of harassment, use the horn to attract attention. Try to find a safe and public place, such as a police station, hotel, or gas station. Make sure embassy drivers are trained in defensive driving.

Never stop for hitchhikers or people lying on the road. Report the situation to the local police and drive on. Always park in well-lit areas and close to exit doors, leaving all valuables locked in the trunk.

Conclusion

Times have changed, but some age-old practices remain the same. This has never been more evident than now, when travel is so accessible and people move around more than ever, for both business and pleasure, meeting people from all over the world. People now find themselves in new situations or in the company of people from new cultures, which is something they may never have encountered before. Along with the broadening of geographical horizons comes the need to know how to behave appropriately in a new situation. What was previously, in the main, part of a diplomat's life as they moved around the world has now become a reality for the average person. Knowing some basic rules of protocol and etiquette can be extremely useful.

Bibliography

Amaral, Isabel, *Imagem e Internacionalização*: Editorial Verbo, 2000

Arruda, Fabio, *Sempre, às vezes, nunca*: Editora ARX, 2003

le Bras, Florence, *Le guide du Savoir Vivre*: Marabout, 2004

Cunha, H. de Mendonça e, *Regras do Cerimonial Português*: Livraria Bertrand, 1976

Gandouin, Jacques, *Guide du protocole et des usages*: Editions Stock, 1995

Lydeka, Arminas, *Etiketas Kievienam*: Eugrimas, 2004

Mantoux, Thierry, *BCBG Le Guide du bon chich bon genre*: Editions Hermé, 1985

Post, Peggy, *Emily's Post Etiquette*: Perfect bound, 2004

Serrano, José de Bouza, *Apontamentos sobre atendimento, imprensa e protocolo*: Ministério de Comércio e Turismo, 1979

Index